APEX PREDATORS

TIGER

E. Melanie Watt

AV2

www.openlightbox.com

AV2

Step 1
Go to **www.openlightbox.com**

Step 2
Enter this unique code

TAKNBQMHL

Step 3
Explore your interactive eBook!

AV2 is optimized for use on any device

Your interactive eBook comes with...

Contents
Browse a live contents page to easily navigate through resources

Audio
Listen to sections of the book read aloud

Videos
Watch informative video clips

Weblinks
Gain additional information for research

Slideshows
View images and captions

Try This!
Complete activities and hands-on experiments

Key Words
Study vocabulary, and complete a matching word activity

Quizzes
Test your knowledge

Share
Share titles within your Learning Management System (LMS) or Library Circulation System

Citation
Create bibliographical references following APA, CMOS, and MLA styles

This title is part of our AV2 digital subscription

1-Year Grades K–5 Subscription
ISBN 978-1-7911-3320-7

Access hundreds of AV2 titles with our digital subscription.
Sign up for a FREE trial at **www.openlightbox.com/trial**

The digital components of this book are guaranteed to stay active for at least five years from the date of publication.

APEX PREDATORS

TIGER

CONTENTS

2 AV2 Book Code
4 The Tiger
6 All about Roaring Cats
8 Tiger Physical Features
10 Tiger Habitats
12 Lone Cats
14 Tiger Life Cycle
16 On the Hunt
18 Tiger Conservation
20 Tigers and People
21 Myths and Legends
22 Tiger Quiz
23 Key Words/Index

The Tiger

The tiger is the largest type of cat in the world. These **mammals** are easily recognized by the dark stripes in their fur. They are mostly found in Asia, but are well-known worldwide. As powerful **predators**, tigers hunt a variety of **prey** using their sharp teeth and claws. Their prey includes deer, boars, and water buffalo.

Tigers, like many other large **carnivores**, are apex predators. This means that they eat other animals and rarely have natural predators of their own. Apex predators, including the tiger, are typically **keystone species**. This means that their presence has a large effect on their surrounding area. For example, their prey changes behavior to avoid them. Apex predators also serve an important **ecosystem** role, as they may stop certain types of prey from growing too large in number and damaging the **environment**.

Throughout history, tigers have been both worshiped and feared. Today, with large amounts of tiger **habitat** destroyed, and many tigers killed by humans, conservation programs are working hard to save them. Tigers rely on continued international cooperation to help reverse this human-caused pattern of loss.

SPEEDY SPRINTING

Tigers can **run** up to **40 miles** (65 kilometers) **per hour** for short distances.

All about Roaring Cats

There are about 40 wild cat species in the world. Of these, only tigers, lions, jaguars, and leopards can roar. Unlike most other cats, a roaring cat has a stretchy **ligament** in its voice box. This causes the cat to roar instead of purr. Each roaring cat species has a long tail, strong legs, a flexible spine, sharp claws, large teeth, and powerful jaws.

Roaring cats can vary greatly in weight. The heaviest are from a tiger **population** that lives in eastern Russia and northeastern China. They are known as Amur, or Siberian, tigers. Amur tigers weigh more than the second-largest roaring cats, lions. The smallest tigers, found in Sumatra, only weigh about half as much as Amur tigers. Leopards are the smallest, lightest roaring cats.

Tigers only live in Asia, while lions and leopards live in both Africa and Asia. Jaguars are the only roaring cats found in North and South America. Roaring cats live in many types of habitats, including forests, grasslands, and mountains.

THINK ABOUT IT

How are the diets of roaring cats similar among the species? In what ways would their diets vary from species to species? What are some reasons for these similarities and differences?

In addition to their smaller size, Sumatran tigers are also known for having thicker "beards" and manes than other types of tigers.

Comparing Roaring Cats

All roaring cats have certain characteristics, but they also have a wide range of different physical features, habitats, and diets. Due to their distinctive coats, tigers are rarely confused with other roaring cats.

Tiger *(Panthera tigris)*

- **Average Body Length**: 7 to 12 feet (2.1 to 3.7 meters)
- **Average Weight**: 165 to 715 pounds (75 to 324 kilograms)
- **Habitat**: forests, grasslands, savannas, shrublands, tundra, wetlands
- **Diet**: small animals, **carrion**, large mammals, including deer, wild pigs, and water buffalo

Lion *(Panthera leo)*

- **Average Body Length**: 5 to 8 feet (1.5 to 2.4 m)
- **Average Weight**: 243 to 600 pounds (110 to 272 kg)
- **Habitat**: deserts, forests, savannas
- **Diet**: small animals, carrion, medium-to-large hoofed mammals, including antelopes and zebras

Jaguar *(Panthera onca)*

- **Average Body Length**: 4 to 6 feet (1.2 to 1.8 m)
- **Average Weight**: 150 to 300 pounds (68 to 136 kg)
- **Habitat**: forests, savannas, scrublands, wetlands
- **Diet**: birds, fish, hoofed mammals, small mammals, reptiles, carrion

Leopard *(Panthera pardus)*

- **Average Body Length**: 3 to 6 feet (0.9 to 1.8 m)
- **Average Weight**: 38 to 198 pounds (17 to 90 kilograms)
- **Habitat**: deserts, forests, mountains, savannas, scrublands
- **Diet**: birds, fish, small mammals, reptiles, carrion, medium hoofed mammals, such as gazelles

Tiger

Physical Features

Tigers, like all living things, have unique **adaptations** that help them survive in their habitat. Many of these adaptations are physical, or part of the animal's body. Some of these features help a tiger hunt, while others help it survive in its environment in other ways.

TAIL

A tiger's tail is about 3 feet (0.9 m) long. It helps the cat balance while chasing prey or climbing. The tail is also used to communicate with other tigers. Rapidly moving the tail from side to side, or keeping it low while intensely twitching it, is a sign of aggression.

LEGS

A tiger's back, or hind, legs are longer than its front legs. This allows it to leap as far as 33 feet (10 m) by using them to push off the ground. A tiger can also use its legs to easily swim more than 18 miles (29 km) in a single day.

EYES

A tiger's eyes face forward and focus on one object, giving the cat what is known as binocular vision. This means tigers can accurately determine distances and depth, helping them pounce on prey. Tiger eyes are adapted to see in the dark by reflecting light. This gives the cats night vision six times better than that of a person.

TEETH

Adult tigers have 30 teeth in their powerful jaws. The teeth near a tiger's cheek cut meat into smaller pieces to swallow. Incisors, small teeth in the front of the mouth, are used to pull meat from bones and for grooming. A tiger's **canine teeth** are larger than those of any other cat species. They can be 3.5 inches (8.9 cm) long and are used to bite, hold, and kill prey.

PAWS

The padded feet of a tiger help it **stalk** prey quietly. A tiger's claws are up to 4 inches (10 centimeters) long and are retracted into the cat's paws when not in use. This helps keep the claws sharp and the tiger's steps silent. The claws come out to help the tiger catch prey or defend itself. The curved shape of a tiger's claws help it grasp its prey and climb trees.

Tiger Habitats

Today, tigers are found only in South and Southeast Asia, China, and Eastern Russia. Some must be able live in tropical locations, with daytime temperatures that can reach 104° Fahrenheit (40° Celsius). Others must survive in the cold and snow of mountainous areas, where temperatures may drop to -40°F (-40°C). Tigers living in warmer areas rest in the shade or in water to avoid the heat, while those in colder climates grow thick coats of fur in winter in order to keep warm.

Tigers need home ranges with plant cover, water, and enough prey to eat. Those living in habitats with large amounts of consistently available prey tend to have smaller home ranges than those in areas with fewer animals to eat. For instance, in parts of Nepal, with large amounts of prey available throughout the year, male tiger home ranges average 11.5 to 40.5 square miles (30 to 105 square km). However, in far eastern Russia, where prey animals such as deer move through large areas with the seasons, tiger home ranges may be as large as 770 square miles (2,000 square km). Young male tigers may travel hundreds of miles (km) or more in order to find a suitable place to use as their home range. A young female tiger will often establish a range near that of her mother.

Although tigers enjoy resting in water, they usually keep their heads above the surface to keep their eyes clear.

Tigers around the World

1 Kaziranga National Park and Tiger Reserve, India

Kaziranga National Park was formed in 1908, and helped save the Indian one-horned rhinoceros from **extinction**. Over time, it also became a **breeding** area for many common tiger prey species. The tiger population in the park increased to the point where it was considered a tiger reserve by 2007. Today, Kaziranga National Park and Tiger Reserve has one of the highest tiger **densities** in India.

2 Point Defiance Zoo & Aquarium, Washington, United States

Point Defiance Zoo & Aquarium participates in a breeding plan for Sumatran tigers. There are fewer than 500 Sumatran tigers left in nature due to **poaching** and habitat loss in the Indonesian island of Sumatra. Breeding programs such as this help keep the population of Sumatran tigers healthy as a whole.

3 Ile-Balkhash Reserve, Kazakhstan

Tigers disappeared from Kazakhstan more than 70 years ago. Many organizations are working together to return tigers to this country by 2025. In the Ile-Balkhash Reserve, habitat improvements and other actions meant to increase the populations of tiger prey species are already underway. A government program aims to restore ecosystems using lessons learned from tiger introduction projects in other countries. In the near future, Ile-Balkhash Reserve may be able to support 120 tigers.

Lone Cats

Tigers usually live alone, except for mothers with young. An adult male and female are only together for about a week to mate. A mother tiger needs a home range large enough to raise her cubs. An adult male tiger's home range often overlaps with the ranges of multiple females. To communicate, tigers use a complex combination of scent marks, visual signals, and sounds. Vocalizations include roars, growls, snarls, grunts, moans, mews, and hisses.

A tiger's roar helps the cat defend its territory by letting other tigers know both where it is and how large it is.

Adult tigers mark their home ranges by leaving scent and visual marks on nearby objects. This includes spraying a smelly fluid, leaving odors created by scent **glands**, and raking the ground or scraping trees with their claws. Together, different forms of tiger communication help each cat provide other tigers with information including its identity, the boundaries of its territory or range, and whether it is ready to mate. This information can help prevent tigers from getting into unwanted encounters or unnecessary fights with each other.

Male tigers may come into conflict with each other over potential mates. The tigers stare, growl, and possibly strike at each other, usually until one backs down.

Tigers curl their top lips and inhale when smelling marks left by each other. Known as flehmen, this behavior helps the cat take in scents more easily.

Tiger

Life Cycle

Female tigers give birth in a sheltered den or nest area. This is often in tall grass or brush, in a cave, or among rocks that the mother may cover with grass, leaves, and fur. Although mothers provide much care for their cubs, life for a young tiger is not easy. Only about half of all cubs reach the age of two. Threats to their survival include predators, adult male tigers, starvation, fires, and flooding. If a female tiger loses all of her cubs, she may have another litter within five months.

1 CUB

A mother tiger usually has two or three cubs in a litter, although she can have up to seven. Newborn cubs only weigh about 1.7 to 3.5 pounds (0.8 to 1.6 kg). They are helpless at birth. Cubs first open their eyes after about a week. Their ears open after about 10 days. The mother is very protective, staying with the cubs and nursing them, only leaving briefly to hunt. If she senses danger, she may carry her cubs, one at a time, to a safer shelter. Once her cubs are about seven weeks old, she begins to bring food back to them. Cubs build up strength by playing with each other. At about two months of age, they start to spend time outside of the den.

2 JUVENILE

When they are about six months old, tigers learn to hunt with their mother. She teaches them to stalk, attack, and kill prey. Juvenile tigers grow quickly. A 1-year-old may weigh 300 pounds (136 kg) or more. By the time they are 2 years of age, young tigers become independent and leave their mother to find home ranges of their own.

3 ADULT

Female tigers are considered adults, and can have young of their own, when they are three or four years old. Males mature when they are 4 or 5 years old. Male tigers tend to grow larger than female tigers. A tiger's lifespan in nature is about 8 to 15 years, although some individuals can live up to 20 years of age. Tigers can come together to mate at any time during the year, but those living in tropical habitats most often do so during the cooler winter or spring months.

On the Hunt

Although tigers will eat many different types of prey species, most of their diet comes from large hoofed animals. Depending on where the tiger lives, this can include many species of deer, water buffalo, and wild pigs. Tigers living near humans will also eat domestic animals, such as cattle, horses, and goats. These big cats may eat other predators, including brown and black bears, leopards, and crocodiles. On rare occasions, tigers will kill very large prey, such as Indian elephants or young Indian rhinoceroses. If large prey is not available, these big cats will feed on smaller animals, including rodents and fish. In some cases, tigers have also been known to prey on humans.

Tigers tend to hunt in the evening, night, and early morning. They hunt alone most of the time. A tiger's vertical stripes help the cat **camouflage** itself by breaking up its shape as it moves silently using brush, trees, and rocks for cover. Tigers usually **ambush** their prey by leaping onto it after stalking it. Small prey is killed with a bite to the back of its neck. Large prey is killed by a bite to the throat. This helps the tiger avoid any antlers or horns.

Many tiger prey species cannot see orange and green as separate colors. This means that a tiger's fur can help it hide among plants to stalk prey more easily.

THINK ABOUT IT

Tigers are known to eat other predatory animals, such as bears. What advantages might they have that allow them to do this successfully?

After prey has been killed, the tiger carries or drags its meal to cover. There, it may feed for days, eating 40 to 110 pounds (18 to 50 kg) of meat at a time. If the tiger must go to water or another resting place, it often covers its kill with leaves, dirt, and grass. This keeps the meal safe for when the tiger returns. Hunting is not easy, and tigers are not able to eat every day. Depending on the type of tiger, these cats may travel 10 to 37 miles (16 to 60 km) in a day searching for prey. Although tigers are powerful predators, their prey is often fast and alert. For each successful hunt a tiger makes, about 20 attempts fail.

Energy Pyramid

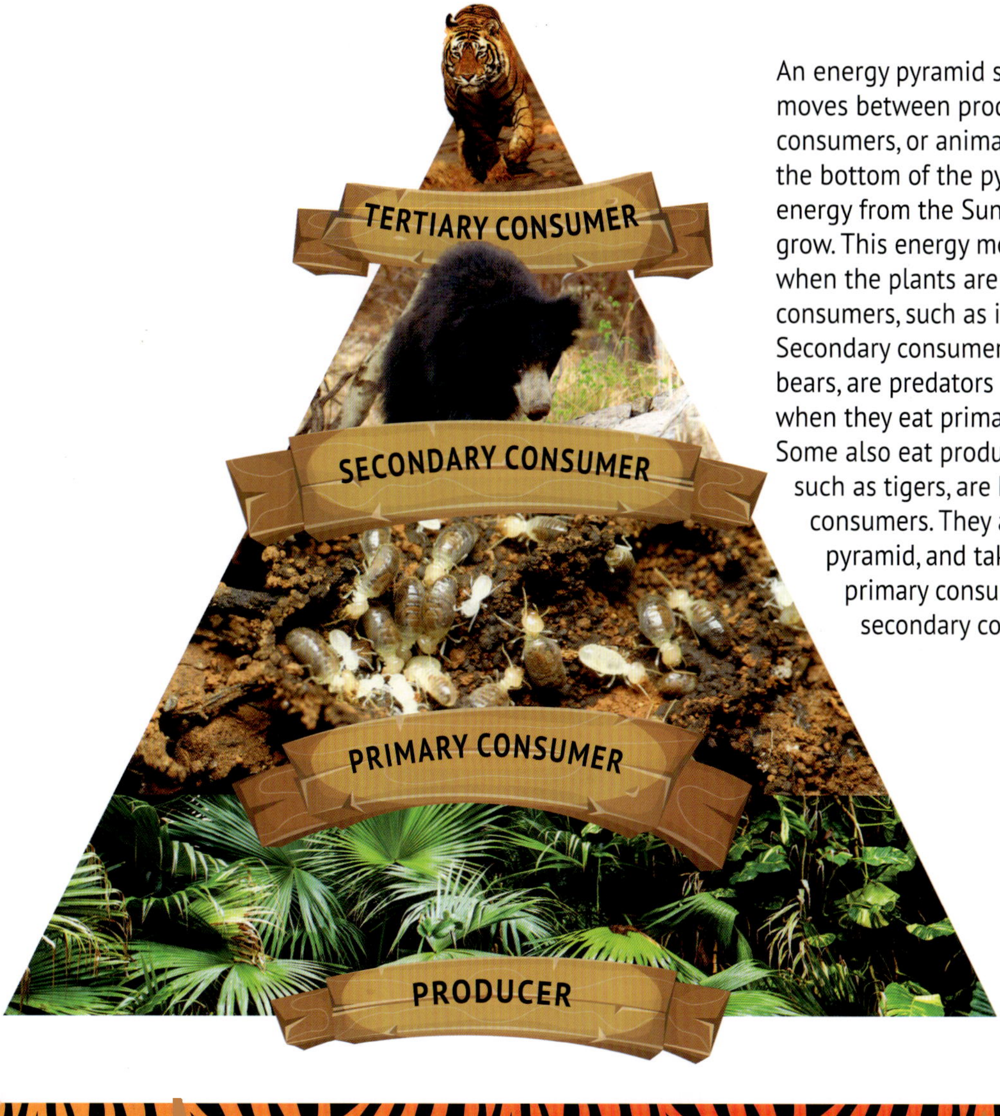

An energy pyramid shows how energy moves between producers, or plants, and consumers, or animals. Producers are at the bottom of the pyramid. They take energy from the Sun's light and use it to grow. This energy moves up the pyramid when the plants are eaten by primary consumers, such as insects and deer. Secondary consumers, including sloth bears, are predators that take energy when they eat primary consumers. Some also eat producers. Apex predators, such as tigers, are known as tertiary consumers. They are at the top of the pyramid, and take energy by eating primary consumers as well as secondary consumers.

Tiger Conservation

Although tigers are powerful apex predators, the species is fighting for survival. In little more than 100 years, the number of tigers in nature has decreased from about 100,000 to an estimated 3,500–5,500. Meanwhile, about 93 percent of the world's tiger habitat has disappeared. During this time, humans have been the largest threat to tigers, mainly by hunting them and destroying their habitats. This has continued in recent years. Today, more than 60 percent of remaining tiger populations are found in protected areas.

As their habitats have decreased, tiger populations have become separated from each other by obstacles such as towns and roads. This has made it harder for them to find mates.

People from local, regional, national, and international groups are working together to protect and increase tiger populations. Activities include reducing poaching and human-wildlife conflict, improving protected area management, and restoring habitats and the natural connections between them. Local communities are also involved in land-use planning, raising tiger awareness, and developing jobs that do not harm the environment in areas near critical tiger habitats. Some areas, using a combination of these methods, have already shown increases in tiger numbers.

Tiger Status

Tigers have been considered an **endangered** species for a long time. Currently, tiger populations are found only in scattered areas in Asia. Most are found in India. Several countries have lost their tiger populations completely in the last few decades. In spite of laws in place to help protect tigers in most areas where they live, poaching and habitat loss are still leading to decreased numbers in some countries.

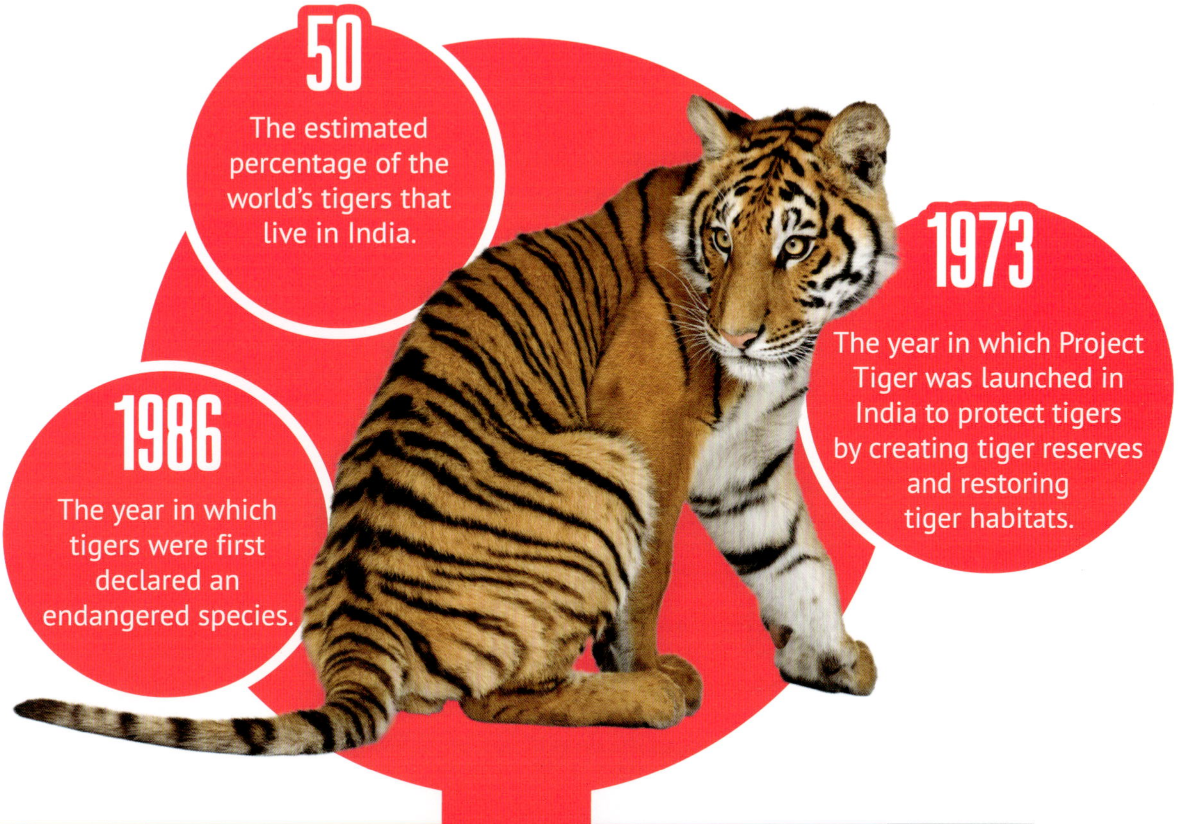

LEAST CONCERN	NEAR THREATENED	VULNERABLE	ENDANGERED	CRITICALLY ENDANGERED	EXTINCT IN THE WILD	EXTINCT

Tigers and People

Throughout history, humans and tigers have often been in conflict. Tigers have killed more humans than any other cat species. In one case, a single tiger had killed more than 400 people by the time it was hunted down in 1907. At that time, about 1,000 people per year were killed by tigers in India. In recent years, steps have been taken to reduce human-tiger conflicts. Between 2015 and 2018, the Indian government reported that an average of 34 people were killed in the country by tigers each year.

Humans kill tigers as well. Between 1875 and 1925, more than 80,000 tigers were reported to have been killed in India. Today, people continue to illegally kill tigers for their fur and other body parts. These are sold at high prices for use in traditional medicines and to collectors. People also hunt tigers in response to attacks on people or livestock.

Although humans and tigers may harm each other, the animals have long been considered important in many cultures. Today, tigers are popular animals worldwide. Many people travel to zoos and parks to see them.

Tigers often attack their prey from behind. In the Sundarbans, a mangrove forest area on the border of India and Bangladesh, fishers and other people who work outdoors may wear masks on the backs of their heads in an effort to prevent these attacks.

MYTHS AND LEGENDS

At one time, tigers were found in a multitude of countries. The people in each of these countries both feared and honored these predators. They created many myths about tigers. In some stories, humans and other animals trick tigers in order to save themselves. This includes several tales of how the tiger got his stripes. In one version, told in Vietnam, a tiger wondered why a big buffalo was working for a man who was so much weaker than it. The tiger thought the reason must be the man's wisdom, so he demanded that the man give him some. The man was very afraid, but convinced the tiger to let him tie the cat up while he went home to get his wisdom. However, the man did not come back. The tiger struggled so hard getting out of his ropes that he developed dark stripes on his fur. The tiger still hides in the shadows to this day, searching for wisdom.

Each year of the Chinese calendar is represented by 1 of 12 animals. According to legend, people born in the year of a specific animal may have features of that animal. People born in the year of the tiger are thought to be independent, brave, heroic, strong, and full of energy. The last year of the tiger started in 2022, and the next will start in 2034.

Tiger Quiz

1 Which species of cats can roar?

2 How fast can a tiger run?

3 How far can a tiger leap?

4 Which location in India has one of the highest tiger densities in the world?

5 How many cubs does a mother tiger usually have in a litter?

6 At what age does a young tiger leave its mother to find its own home range?

7 For each successful hunt a tiger makes, how many are unsuccessful?

8 How do tigers communicate with each other?

ANSWERS: 1. The tiger, lion, jaguar, and leopard **2.** Up to 40 miles per hour (65 kph) for short distances **3.** Up to 33 feet (10 m) **4.** Kaziranga National Park and Tiger Reserve **5.** Two or three **6.** At about 2 years of age **7.** About 20 **8.** With scent marks, visual signals, and sounds

Key Words

adaptations: physical features or behaviors that help an animal survive in its habitat

ambush: attack from hiding

breeding: coming together to have young

camouflage: to hide by blending into one's surroundings

canine teeth: four cone-shaped, pointed teeth located beside the front incisors

carnivores: animals that eat mostly or only meat

carrion: dead and rotting animals

densities: the amounts of things within a certain area

ecosystem: living things interacting with each other and with their environment

endangered: in danger of no longer existing anywhere on Earth

environment: the plants, animals, and other natural features of an area

extinction: the state of no longer being alive anywhere on Earth

glands: parts of an animal's body that create substances such as saliva or sweat

habitat: a place where a plant or animal lives in nature

keystone species: a group of animals needed to keep their habitat in balance. Like other species, the animals in a keystone species shares similar features and can reproduce with each other.

ligament: a stretchy band of tissue connected to a bone or organ

mammals: warm-blooded animals that have hair or fur and nurse their young

poaching: the illegal killing, trapping or taking of wildlife

population: a group of individuals of the same species living and interbreeding within a given area

predators: animals that live by killing other animals for food

prey: animals that are hunted by other animals for food

stalk: follow quietly in order to catch or kill prey

Index

claws 4, 6, 9, 13
cubs 12, 14, 22

eyes 9, 10, 14

Ile-Balkhash Reserve 11

jaguars 6, 7, 22
juveniles 15

Kaziranga National Park and Tiger Reserve 11, 22

legs 6, 8
leopards 6, 7, 16, 22
lions 6, 7, 22

paws 9
Point Defiance Zoo & Aquarium 11

stripes 4, 16, 21

tail 6, 8
teeth 4, 6, 9

Get the best of both worlds.

AV2 bridges the gap between print and digital.

The expandable resources toolbar enables quick access to content including **videos**, **audio**, **activities**, **weblinks**, **slideshows**, **quizzes**, and **key words**.

Animated videos make static images come alive.

Resource icons on each page help readers to further **explore key concepts**.

Published by Lightbox Learning Inc.
276 5th Avenue
Suite 704 #917
New York, NY 10001
Website: www.openlightbox.com

Library of Congress Control Number: 2023941647

ISBN 978-1-7911-5675-6 (hardcover)
ISBN 978-1-7911-5676-3 (softcover)
ISBN 978-1-7911-5677-0 (multi-user eBook)

Printed in Guangzhou, China
1 2 3 4 5 6 7 8 9 0 27 26 25 24 23

072023
101122

Project Coordinator: John Willis
Designer: Terry Paulhus

Photo Credits
Every reasonable effort has been made to trace ownership and to obtain permission to reprint copyright material. The publisher would be pleased to have any errors or omissions brought to its attention so that they may be corrected in subsequent printings.
The publisher acknowledges Alamy, Bridgeman Pictures, Getty Images, and Minden Pictures as its primary image suppliers for this title.